POTATO DISHES
FOR ALL
OCCASIONS

POTATO DISHES

FOR ALL
OCCASIONS

Melinda Migale

authorHOUSE®

AuthorHouse™
1663 Liberty Drive
Bloomington, IN 47403
www.authorhouse.com
Phone: 1-800-839-8640

Published by AuthorHouse   01/16/2013

ISBN: 978-1-4817-0528-8 (sc)
ISBN: 978-1-4817-0527-1 (e)

Library of Congress Control Number: 2013900443

Any people depicted in stock imagery provided by Thinkstock are models, and such images are being used for illustrative purposes only.
Certain stock imagery © Thinkstock.

This book is printed on acid-free paper.

Because of the dynamic nature of the Internet, any web addresses or links contained in this book may have changed since publication and may no longer be valid. The views expressed in this work are solely those of the author and do not necessarily reflect the views of the publisher, and the publisher hereby disclaims any responsibility for them.

CONTENTS

3. Steamed Potatoes

4. Cooked Potatoes

5. Fried Potatoes

6. Baked Potatoes

7. Sweet Potatoes

8. Potato Sauces

1. INTRODUCTION.

This book is intended to show the advantages of cooking with potatoes. There are few vegetables as versatile as the potato, which can be prepared in many ways in all kinds of tasty and healthy dishes.

Potatoes can be served with meats, mushrooms, fish, and vegetables. They can be boiled, fried, baked, grated, milled, scalloped, steamed, or filled with other ingredients.

Potatoes are native to North and South America and were introduced to Europe in the sixteenth century. In Spain, potatoes were first planted as decorative plants.

In the eighteenth century, Europeans began eating potatoes, and they became an important food source throughout the world. Nowadays, all countries plant potatoes for food and for decoration.

Potatoes are an important source of nutrition, as they contain minerals, including magnesium, calcium, phosphorus, and potassium, and micronutrients, including zinc, boron, cobalt, manganese, nickel, and iron. They also contain vitamins C, E, and K and B vitamins, along with sugars and other carbohydrates important for health.

2. Equipment.

Baking Pan Liners
Parchment paper, available in rolls and sheets, can be cut to fit any size baking sheet, and it makes an excellent nonstick surface for baking all kinds of potato cookies, pastries, pancakes, and breads. I like reusable silicone sheets even better, especially for cookies. Silpat is one popular brand of silicone sheets.

When using a baking pan liner, there's no need to grease the sheet with butter or cooking spray. Simply lay the liner on your baking sheet, and when you're through, simply throw the parchment away or wash the silicone sheet in warm water and then rinse and dry it.

Baking Sheets
These come in rimmed and rimless versions. Rimmed sheets can be used for rolls, pancakes, and cookies. For cooking in batches, it's most convenient to have two of each of the two most common sizes of rimmed baking sheet, 15 1/2 × 10 1/2 × 1 inch or 12 × 18 × 1 inch (the latter is also called a "half sheet pan").

Rimless sheets are designed for baked goods that don't need sides to contain them, such as pastries. Those made from heavy aluminum are many people's favorites, but insulated sheets are also available. These have a layer of air between two layers of aluminum, which prevents burning but increases baking times and can make the texture of pastries or cookies too soft.

Baking Stone
A preheated baking stone gives a jolt of heat to yeast breads, making them rise higher than they would if baked on a baking sheet set on the oven rack.

Baking stones are sold at specialty cookware shops and online. These come in round and rectangular shapes in sizes that fit perfectly on an oven rack with room to spare around the sides.

These take a while to preheat, so plan on turning your oven on about 1 hour before the dough is ready for baking.

Rectangular and Square Baking Pans
Straight-sided pans made of sturdy, durable aluminum with lips that make them easy to grasp with a pot holder without touching the batter are available at www.bakerscatalogue.com and www. bridgekitchenware.com.

You might find lightweight aluminum pans with slightly sloping sides available used, and these work fine too.
Round baking pans, pans, and tube pans are used to make sweet pastries, baked potato baba, and other specialty goods.

Measuring Cups and Spoons
Dry and liquid ingredients must be measured in different kinds of cups. For liquids, use a clear glass heatproof cup with a spout. These come in sizes ranging from 1 cup to 2 quarts.

To measure sticky liquids like molasses, either brush the inside of the cup lightly with flavorless vegetable oil or coat the cup very lightly with cooking spray; the liquid will then slide right out of the cup.

For dry ingredients, you'll need one or two sets of nested heavy stainless steel measuring cups with straight sides, ranging in size from 1/4 cup to 1 cup. To measure dry ingredients, fill the cup and then sweep off any excess with a narrow metal spatula or the straight back of a knife.

Measuring spoons come in sets that usually include 1/4 teaspoon, 1/2 teaspoon, 1 teaspoon, and 1 tablespoon measurements. Heavy stainless steel spoons are best. To use a measuring spoon, dip the spoon into the container, filling it to overflowing, and level it by sweeping off the excess in the same manner as using a measuring cup. When measuring baking soda, cream of tartar, or ground ginger, which tend to clump, break up any lumps first with the spoon before measuring.

Scale

The kitchen scale is extremely useful for those times when you want to be accurate. And when making individual breads or rolls, the matter-to-weight ratio of the dough must be precise so that all will be the same size.

Mixing Equipment

An electric mixer is great for mixing batters and for whipping egg whites or cream. There are several powerful handheld mixers on the market today, adjustable to several speeds. Electric mixers such as those made by Kitchen Aid will cut the time for beating cake batters, whipping egg whites, and kneading heavy dough to mere minutes.

Heatproof Rubber Spatulas

These are very handy for cooking, stirring, and folding batters, especially when mixing flour and egg whites for delicate cake batters.

Mixing Bowls

The following sizes are especially useful: 2 cups, 2 quarts, 4 quarts, and 5 quarts. Stainless steel or glass bowls are best, as plastic bowls tend to hang on to grease, no matter how thoroughly they're washed, which inhibits the stiffening of egg whites.

Whisks

These tools are great for beating and for smoothing out lumpy mixtures such as cornstarch-thickened sauces or pastry cream. A small whisk is useful for mixing small amounts either in a small bowl or a small saucepan. A medium-sized whisk can be used for beating a few eggs or egg whites.

Wooden Spoons

These are useful for stirring batters and sauces.

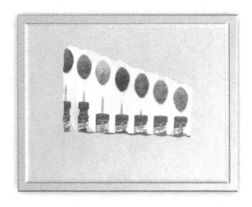

3. USEFUL TIPS FOR COOKING POTATOES

~ All vegetables (except peas and beets) should be cooked in salted water.
~ Peel potatoes and cut them with a stainless steel knife right before cooking.
~ To preserve vitamins, cook veggies in boiling water.
~ To keep potatoes cooked in their peels from becoming mushy, add 1 tablespoon of salt to the boiling water.
~ Potatoes are most easily peeled when sprayed with cold water.
~ To keep potatoes from breaking up during boiling, cook them over medium heat.
~ Add hot milk to potato puree gradually.
~ To keep potatoes from bursting in the oven, prick them with a fork or knife.
~ To keep grated potatoes from turning brown, grate an onion on the same grater first.
~ Potato pancakes will be fluffier if a small amount of baking soda is added to the batter.
~ Potatoes will boil faster if a spoonful of margarine is added to the water.
~ To keep your hands from turning brown when peeling young potatoes, spray the potatoes with vinegar.
~ To keep potatoes from losing minerals and vitamins, boil them for no longer than 15 minutes.

1. Salads

1. Grilled Greek Potato Salad

Ingredients:
3 lbs. small red potatoes, halved
2 Tbsp. olive oil
1/2 tsp. salt
1/4 tsp. pepper
1 large sweet yellow pepper, chopped
1 large sweet red pepper, chopped
1 medium red onion, halved and sliced
1 medium cucumber, chopped
1 1/4 c. grape tomatoes, halved
1/2 lb. fresh mozzarella cheese, cubed
3/4 c. Greek vinaigrette
1/2 c. Greek olives, halved
1 can (2 1/4oz.) sliced ripe olives, drained
2 Tbsp. minced fresh oregano or 1 tsp. dried oregano

Preparation:
1. Drizzle the potatoes with oil and sprinkle with salt and pepper. Toss to coat.
2. Grill potatoes, covered, over medium heat for 20 to 25 minutes or until tender.
3. Place the veggies in a large bowl. Add the remaining ingredients, and toss to coat. Serve warm or cold.

2. Potato Salad with Onion

Ingredients:
5 to 6 potatoes, boiled in peels
2 onions
1/2 c. Salad Dressing (see recipe 10 in chapter 8)
Salt and pepper to taste

Preparation
1. Cut potatoes into rounds.
2. Create simple circled pieces of onion, then cut the onion circles into smaller pieces and grate. Combine with salt and pepper.
3. Mix the potato rounds, onion, and Salad Dressing.

3. Potato Salad with Beans

Ingredients:
4 to 5 medium potatoes
1 large onion,
1 Tbsp. lemon juice or white wine vinegar
1 dash each salt and sugar
1 c. white or black beans
4 to 5 tsp. olive oil
pepper to taste

Preparation:
1. Bring potatoes to a boil in their peels. Allow to cool and cut into thin rounds.
2. Cut onions in half and sprinkle with lemon juice, salt, and sugar.
3. Simmer the beans in a glass pot 4-5 hours before preparation, stirring with a fork, until soft.
4. Drain the beans and combine them with the potatoes and onions.
5. Sprinkle the mixture with olive oil and pepper.

4. German Potato Salad

Ingredients:
4 lbs. small red potatoes, quartered
10 bacon strips, chopped
1 large onion
3 Tbsp. celery, chopped
2 Tbsp. green pepper, chopped
1 Tbsp. all-purpose flour
1 Tbsp. sugar,
1 tsp. salt
1/2 tsp. pepper
1 c. water
1/3 c. white balsamic vinegar

Preparation:
1. Place the potatoes in a Dutch warm oven and cover with water.
2. Bring to a boil. Reduce the heat, cover, and simmer for 15 to 20 minutes or until tender.
3. Meanwhile, in a large skillet, cook bacon over medium heat until crisp.
4. Using a slotted spoon, remove bacon to paper towels.
5. In the bacon drippings, sauté the onion, celery, and green pepper until tender.
6. Stir in the flour, sugar, salt, and pepper. Continue stirring until blended.
7. Combine the water and balsamic vinegar. Stir into the vegetable mixture.
8. Bring the vegetable mixture to a boil. Cook, stir, for 2 minutes or until thickened.
9. Drain the potatoes and place them in a large serving bowl. Pour the vegetable mixture over the potatoes.
10. Add bacon and toss to coat. Serve warm or at room temperature.

5. Potato Salad with Cabbage

Ingredients:
4 to 5 medium potatoes
1 medium onion chopped
1-2 Tbsp. lemon juice
7-8 oz. sour cabbage
1 bunch green parsley, chopped
Salt, sugar, and black pepper to taste
1-2 Tbsp. wine vinegar
2 to 3 Tbsp. olive oil

Preparation:
1. Boil the potatoes in their skins. Drain, cool, and then slice.
2. Soften the onion soften with lemon juice.
3. Combine the potatoes with cabbage and softened onion.
4. Fold in the green parsley. Add salt, sugar, pepper, and vinegar.
5. Add olive oil and mix thoroughly.

6. Potato Salad with Corn and Apples

Ingredients:
3 potatoes, boiled in peels
2 apples
1 can(7-8 oz.) golden corn
1 bunch dill, chopped and divided
1 bunch chives, chopped
1 tsp. salt
4 Tbsp. Salad Dressing (see recipe 10 in chapter 8)

Preparation:
1. Peel the boiled potatoes and cut into small squares.
2. Peel and dice the apples.
3. Drain the corn and blend it with a small amount of chives and the apples.
4. Add the remaining ingredients except the dill and mix.
5. Sprinkle with the remaining chopped dill.

7. Potato Salad with Beef

Ingredients:
4 to 5 potatoes, cooked in peels
7oz. cooked beef
2 to 3 pickled cucumbers
½ can green pea
4 Tbsp. mayo
salt to taste
1 Tbsp. dill

Preparation:
1. Finely dice the potatoes, beef, and pickles and combine them in a bowl.
2. Drain the peas and add them to the bowl.
3. Add the mayo and combine. Add salt to taste and sprinkle with dill.

8. Potato Salad with Pickles

Ingredients:
4 to 5 potatoes, cooked in their peels
3 sour pickles
2 medium onions
3 Tbsp. sour cream
salt.

Preparation:
1. Peel the potatoes.
2. Cut the potatoes, pickles, onions into small squares.
3. Fold in the sour cream, add salt to taste, and gently mix together.

9. Potato Salad with Pickled Peppers

Ingredients:
4 to 5 potatoes, cooked in their peels
2 pickled cucumbers
6-7oz. sweet pickled peppers
1 onion, chopped
1 cooked carrot
4-5oz. green peas
3/4 c. sour cream or mayo
salt to taste

Preparation:
1. Peel the potatoes.
2. Cut the potatoes, carrot, and pickled cucumbers into small chunks. Toss to combine.
3. Add the peas, peppers, and onion.
4. Mix all the ingredients with sour cream.
5. Add salt to taste.

10. Potato Salad with Veggies and Fish

Ingredients:
3 potatoes,
1 cucumber, pickled or fresh
1 large tomato
1 egg, hardboiled
2 fish fillets
7 to 9 green lettuce leaves
1 small onion
1/2 bunch chives
3oz. can green peas, drained
1/2 c. mayo
salt and sugar to taste
1/2 tsp. white or black pepper

Preparation:
1. Boil the potatoes in their peels. Cool and peel from skin.
2. Cut the potatoes, cucumber, tomato, egg, and fish into medium cubes.
3. Chop the lettuce and chives, and cut the onion into small cubes.
4. Add the peas and mayo and mix together.
5. Add the salt, sugar, and pepper to taste.

11. Potato Salad with Wine

Ingredients:
4 to 5 potatoes
1 large carrot, chopped
1 large onion
2 large cloves garlic
½ c. white wine
2 Tbsp. olive oil
1 tsp. 3% vinegar
1/2 tsp. each salt and pepper

Preparation:
1. Bring the potatoes to a boil in their peels.
2. In a separate pot, cook the carrot.
3. Cool the potatoes and cut into small chunks.
4. Cut the onion into small cubes, mince the garlic, and sprinkle each with salt.
5. Thoroughly mix all the vegetables together in a bowl and toss with the wine.
6. Refrigerate the vegetable mixture for approximately 1 hour.
7. When the vegetables have absorbed all the wine, sprinkle the salad with oil, vinegar, salt, and pepper.

12. Potato Salad with Asparagus

Ingredients:
18oz asparagus
16oz. potatoes
1 tsp. cut chives
salt and sugar to taste
1 Tbsp. Mustard Sauce (see recipe 8 in chapter 8)

Preparation:
1. Peel the fibers from the asparagus, rinse with water, and put into boiling water. Add salt and sugar.
2. Cook the asparagus until soft.
3. Cook the potatoes in their peels.
4. Allow the potatoes to cool, and then peel and cut into small chunks.
5. Cut the asparagus into small pieces (approximately 2 cm). Combine with the potato, and add Mustard Sauce.

13. Warm Roasted Red Potato Salad

Ingredients:
One 22oz. package Alexia Olive Oil, Parmesan & Roasted Garlic
Oven Reds
1/2 lb. bag frozen cooked and sliced potatoes
One 5 oz. package salad greens, thoroughly washed
1/2 c. refrigerated blue cheese salad dressing

Preparation:
1. Prepare the potatoes according to the package directions.
2. Just before serving, toss the salad greens with the warm
   potatoes and salad dressing.

2. Soups

1. Zucchini-Potato Soup

Ingredients:
1 medium leek
4 slices bacon
1/2 c. celery, chopped
1 clove garlic, minced
4 c. low-sodium, fat-free chicken broth
1 lb. zucchini (about 3 small squash), sliced
1/2 lb. small new potatoes, quartered
1 c. half-and-half
1/3 c. chopped fresh parsley
1/4 tsp. kosher salt
1/4 tsp. pepper

Preparation:
1. Remove the root, tough outer leaves, and tops from the leek, leaving 2 inches of dark leaves. Slice thinly, rinse well, and drain.
2. Cook the bacon in a large pan over medium-high heat for 8 to 10 minutes or until crisp. Remove from pan and drain on paper towels. Reserving 2 Tbsp. drippings in a Dutch oven. Crumble the bacon.
3. Sauté the leek, celery, and garlic in hot bacon drippings for 3 to 4 minutes or until tender. Add the chicken broth, zucchini, and potatoes, and simmer for 20 to 25 minutes. Stir in the half-and-half, parsley, salt, and pepper. Remove from the heat, and let cool for 5 minutes.
4. Process the potato mixture in batches in a blender or food processor until smooth, stopping to scrape down the sides as needed. Sprinkle with crumbled bacon and serve immediately, or if desired, cover and chill for 4 to 6 hours.

2. Potato Broth

Ingredients:
4 potatoes
1 stalk celery
1 parsley root
1 onion
2 full cups water
2 carrots
2 Tbsp. tomato paste
2 Tbsp. olive oil
1/2 gal. prepared oats
Salt
1 small bunch dill, chopped
1 small bunch parsley, chopped

Preparation:
1. Wash the potatoes, celery, and parsley root and cut into squares.
2. Cut the onion into small cubes and sauté with olive oil.

3. Add the celery and parsley root to the pan, pour in the water, and simmer cook for 45 minutes. 4. Add the potatoes and cook until soft.
4. Add the tomato paste and hot oats.
5. Salt to taste. Garnish with freshly chopped dill and green parsley.

3. Potato Soup with garlic

Ingredients:
7 to 8 potatoes
3 freshly minced garlic cloves
1/2 tsp. salt
3/4 c. milk
1 egg yolk
2 Tbsp. butter
Green herbs, chopped

Preparation:
1. Peel the potatoes and cook in salted water.
2. Grate the cooked potato finely. Add minced garlic and salt.
3. Return the potato mixture to the pot.
4. Cook for10 minutes.
5. Combine the egg yolk with milk and butter. Fold the mixture into the potatoes.
6. Garnish with green herbs and serve warm.

4. Potato Bean Soup

Ingredients:
1 cup butter or black beans
1 gal. chicken, beef, or pork bouillon
8 potatoes, finely diced
2 Tbsp. butter
1 onion
1 carrot
1/2 tsp. salt
1/2 tsp. pepper
1 bay leaf
1 small bunch green herbs

Preparation:
1. Wash the beans and soak in cold water for 3 hours.
2. Drain the beans and add to a pot with the bouillon. Cook on low heat until beans are softened, 1 to 2 hours.
3. Add potatoes and sauté with butter, carrot, and onion. Add to the beans.
4. Add salt, black pepper, and bay leaf. Cook until the vegetables are soft.
5. Garnish with green herbs. Basil, cilantro, parsley, mint, and dill are good additions, or you can choose another herb that you like.

5. Potato Cream with Toasted Bread

Soup

Ingredients:
Meat bouillon;
500 g beef with bones
Greens;
2 onions
3 carrots
2 finely chopped parsley roots
1 small leek
1 stalk celery
1 1/2 potato
1 tsp. butter
1/2 small bunch parsley, chopped
salt

Preparation:

1. Boil the greens and beef in the water to create a bouillon. When soft remove the bones.
2. Peel the potatoes and boil in a separate pot.
3. When the potatoes are hot, grate them finely. Fold in the butter and beef bouillon. Stir until thick.
4. Garnish with chopped green parsley or another herb you like. Salt to the taste. Serve warm.

Toasted Bread:

Ingredients:
1 loaf French bread
1 Tbsp. butter.

Preparation:
1. Remove the crust and cut the bread into cubes or slices.
2. Heat the butter in a saucepan and add the bread.
3. Sauté the bread until lightly browned.

6. Potato Cream with Fried Bread

Soup

Ingredients:
1 carrot, chopped
1 parsley root, chopped
1/2 leek, chopped
1 onion, chopped
2 bay leaves
5 black peppercorns
1/2 tsp. salt
6 to 7 medium potatoes, peeled
1/2 c. sour cream

Preparation:
1. Cook the carrot, parsley root, leek, and onion along with the bay leaves, peppercorns, and herbs in salted water.
2. Add the peeled potatoes to the water.
3. When soft, remove the potatoes and grate finely.
4. Return the potatoes to the pot with the vegetables and broth.
5. Fold in sour cream and heat gently. Do not boil.
6. Serve in small cups with fried bread.

Fried Bread

Ingredients:
1 loaf French bread
100 g cheddar cheese
1 egg yolk
1Tbsp. butter

Preparation:
1. Remove the crusts from the bread and cut into small slices.
2. Grate the cheese and mix with the egg yolk and butter.
3. Spread the cheese mixture on the bread and toast in a warm oven for 5 to 10 minutes or until brown.

7. Potato Cream with Scallion

Ingredients:
5 to 6 potatoes
1 stalk celery, chopped
1 leek, chopped
1 c. plain yogurt
3 c. 2% milk,
1 bunch scallions
1/2 tsp. pepper
1/2 tsp. salt

Preparation:
1. Peel the potato and chop into small squares. Combine with the celery and leek.
2. Boil the veggies in salted water until softened.
3. Drain the vegetables and tear in blender with salt and pepper.
4. Combine the vegetables with milk and heat. Chill in the refrigerator.
5. Before serving, lightly fold in the yogurt and chopped scallion. Great during warm weather.

8. Diet Potato Cream

Ingredients:
7 to 8 potatoes
1 c. water
2 c. milk
2 Tbsp. butter
salt to the taste.
4 Tbsp. carrot juice

Preparation:
1. Peel the potatoes. Add to a pot with cold water and cook until soft.
2. Remove the potatoes and reserve the water.
3. Grate the potatoes. Return the potatoes to the pot and add the reserved water and milk.
4. Add butter and salt and heat.
5. Just before serving, stir in the carrot juice.

9. Diet Potato Cream with Rice

Ingredients:
4 to 5 potatoes
1/2 c. rice
1 carrot
4 Tbsp. butter
2 c. milk
1 egg yolk
salt

Preparation:
1. Cook the potatoes, rice, and carrot separately.
2. Grate the potato and carrot.
3. Warm the milk and add to grated veggies. Stir in the cooked rice.
4. Stir in egg yolk, butter.
5. Serve with warm bread.

10. Potato Cream with Beans

Ingredients:
1/2 c. beans
5 potatoes
2 c. cooked beef bouillon
1 onion
2 Tbsp. butter
1/2 tsp. salt
2 eggs yolks
1/2 c. heavy cream,
Green herbs

Preparation:
1. Cover the beans with water and cook.
2. Peel the potato and cook separately.
3. Grate the potatoes and beans.
4. Combine the potatoes and beans with the bouillon.
5. Chop the onion into small cubes and sauté in butter.
6. Add onions and salt to the soup and cook.
7. Combine the egg yolks and heavy cream into a paste and add to the soup.
8. Garnish with herbs.

11. Potato Cream with Tomatoes

Ingredients:
6 potatoes
4 tomatoes
1/2 gal cooked beef bouillon
2 Tbsp. oil
Salt
1 bunch dill, scallions, or parsley

Preparation:
1. Peel the potatoes and cook in salted water. Drain and grate.
2. Cook the tomatoes in salted water, drain, and grate finely.
3. Combine the potatoes and tomatoes and add bouillon and olive oil. If necessary, reduce the liquid over low heat to thicken the soup.
4. Serve with chopped fresh dill, scallions, or parsley.

12. Potato Soup with Dumplings

Ingredients:
8 potatoes
1 carrot
1 onion
1 parsley root
1/2 gal beef bouillon
2 Tbsp. butter
1 bay leaf
1/2 tsp. each pepper and salt

For the dumplings:
5 Tbsp. oats,
1 Tbsp. butter
2 Tbsp. water
1 egg

Preparation:
1. Peel and dice the potatoes and boil in the bouillon.
2. Grate the carrots, onion, and parsley root. Sauté them in butter and add them to the warm bouillon.
3. Simmer for 15 minutes on low heat.
4. Mix the dumpling ingredients into the dough. Form the dough into tablespoon-sized balls and drop into warm bouillon. Add the bay leaf, pepper, and salt.
5. Boil for another 5 to 10 minutes.

13. Potato Soup from New Potatoes

Ingredients:
1/2 lb. veggies (carrot, leek, onion parsley root, celery, cabbage)
8 new potatoes
2 Tbsp. flour
3 Tbsp. sour cream
1 bunch fresh dill or scallion, chopped
Salt
Pepper
Oregano
Basil

Preparation:
1. Wash veggies, cut onto small chunks, and boil in salted water until softened. Reserve 1/2 cup of the cooking liquid, leaving the rest in the pot, and remove the vegetables.
2. Peel potatoes and cut into chunks. Add to the cooking liquid in the pot and simmer on low heat.
3. Five minutes before the potatoes are done, in a small bowl, mix the flour, the sour cream, and the reserved 1/2 cup of cooking liquid and mix until the flour is dissolved.
4. Stir the flour mixture into the soup with the potatoes, add the reserved vegetables, and warm.
5. Stir in the dill or scallion, and add salt, pepper, oregano, and basil to taste.

14. Spicy Potato Soup

Ingredients:
5 potatoes
1 onion, chopped
1 Tbsp. olive oil
1 Tbsp. flour
1/4 Tbsp. crushed red pepper
50 g bacon
1/2 gal vegetable bouillon
2 Tbsp. tomato paste
1/2 tsp. salt

Preparation:
1. Peel and boil the potatoes. When soft, let cool; then grate on the large holes of a box grater.
2. Sauté the onion in the olive oil. Combine with the grated potatoes.
3. In a small bowl, mix the flour and the red pepper.
4. Cut the bacon into small slices and sauté. Add the spiced flour.
5. Bring the vegetable bouillon to a boil. Add the potato-onion mixture and the bacon.
6. In the sauté pan, combine the tomato paste with a small amount of water and heat, stirring. Stir into the vegetable bouillon.
7. Salt to taste and serve.

15. Potato Soup with Hot Dogs

Ingredients:
1 carrot
2 onions
1 tomato
1/2 stick of celery
1 1/2 gal water
6 potatoes, cut into chunks
1 bay leaf
1/2 tsp. each pepper and salt.
2 hot dogs, cooked and cut into small pieces
2 Tbsp. flour
2 Tbsp. butter

Preparation:
1. Peel and wash the vegetables and cut into small cubes. Sauté in a small amount of butter.
2. Bring the water to a boil. Add the vegetables.
3. Sauté the potatoes in a small amount of butter and add to the vegetables.
4. Add bay leaf, pepper, and salt.
5. Before the water comes to a boil again, add the hot dogs.
6. Cream the flour and butter. Add to the soup and bring to a boil.

16. Potato Soup with Fish

Ingredients:
1 carrot, peeled and diced
1/2 stick celery, peeled and diced
2 onions, grated
2 Tbsp. butter or margarine
1 1/2 c. water
7 potatoes
1 fish
1 bay leaf
1 tomato, chopped
Pepper and salt
Green herbs

Preparation:
1. Sauté the carrot, celery, and onion in the butter or margarine until the vegetables are soft.
2. Bring the water to a boil and add the carrot, celery, and onion. Simmer on low heat for 15 minutes.
3. Cut the potatoes and fish into thin strips. Add to the vegetables and cook until the potatoes are soft.
4. Stir in the bay leaf and tomato.
5. Add salt and pepper to taste.
6. Garnish with green herbs.

17. Potato Soup with Macaroni Noodles

Ingredients:
8 potatoes
1/2 c. macaroni
1 1/2 c. beef stock
Salt
2 Tbsp. butter
1 egg yolk
1/3 c. sour cream
Fresh green herbs, chopped

Preparation:
1. Cook the macaroni. Drain and set aside.
2. Boil the potatoes and mash with a potato masher.
3. In a pot, stir the beef stock into the mashed potatoes. Add the noodles and salt to taste. Cook until warm.
4. Combine the butter, egg yolk, and sour cream. Stir into the other ingredients. Garnish with green herbs.

3. Steamed Potatoes

1. Potato with Bacon and Dried Plums

Ingredients:
200 g lightly smoked bacon
2 onions, finely diced
1 Tbsp. vegetable shortening
10 potatoes
1 c. beef stock
10 dried plums

Bay leaf
Pepper to taste
Salt to the taste.

Preparation:
1. Cut the bacon into small slices and then lightly sauté. Drain and set aside.
2. Sauté the onion in the vegetable shortening.
3. Cut the potatoes into small cubes. Add the potatoes, bacon, and onions to a pot.
4. Add the remaining ingredients to the pot. Simmer on low heat until the potatoes are soft.

2. Potato Filled with Mushrooms

Ingredients:
5 to 6 dried mushrooms
1 leek, chopped
5 Tbsp. butter, divided
1 egg
2 to 3 Tbsp. bread crumbs
15 medium potatoes
1 1/2 c. beef stock
1/2 tsp. each salt, pepper, green herbs

Preparation:
1. Rehydrate the mushrooms in boiling water and then cut into pieces.
2. Sauté the leek in 1 tablespoon of the butter. Add the mushrooms to the sauté pan and heat until leeks are soft.
3. In a small bowl, combine the egg with the bread crumbs. Stir into the mushrooms and leeks and set the mixture aside.
4. Peel fresh potatoes. To cut tops off the potatoes, cut them lengthwise approximately at approximately 1/6 of their height. Set the tops aside.
5. Hollow out the potatoes with a spoon. Fill the hollow with the prepared mushroom mixture and cover with the potato tops.
6. Place the potatoes close together in a pan. Pour the beef stock around the potatoes into the pan and add the rest of the ingredients to the stock.
7. Cover the pan and steam over low heat until the potatoes are soft.

3. Potato Filled with Barley

Ingredients:
8 potatoes
2 Tbsp. barley
1 Tbsp. olive oil
1 onion, minced
1 egg
1 Tbsp. butter
1 c. beef stock
1/2 tsp. salt, pepper
1/2 c. Light Red Sauce (see recipe 9 in chapter 8)
Chopped parsley

Preparation:
1. Peel the potatoes and boil in salted water for several minutes.
2. Drain the potatoes and scoop out a hollow in each one with a spoon.
3. Wash the barley and sauté in the olive oil into light brown.
4. Add warm salted water. Boil and stir until the barley is cooked through.
5. Sauté the onion in the butter, then season with salt and pepper.
6. Add the onion and egg to the barley. Blend thoroughly.
7. Fill the potatoes with the onion-barley batter.
8. Set the potatoes close together in a pan. Pour the stock around the potatoes in the pan and cover. Steam over low heat until the potatoes are soft.
9. Serve with Light Red Sauce and garnish with chopped parsley.

4. Potato Filled with Beef

Ingredients:
9oz. beef (or another meat you like)
Herbs (basil, chives, rosemary, marjoram, or thyme)
2 Tbsp. bread crumbs
8 potatoes
6 Tbsp. olive oil
3 Tbsp. sour cream
Fresh dill or parsley, chopped.

Preparation:
1. Steam the beef head. Combine with the herbs and the bread crumbs and set aside.
2. Boil the potatoes gently in their skins.
3. Allow the potatoes to cool. Cut them in half and scoop out their insides with a spoon.
4. Fill the potatoes with the beef head mixture.
5. Place the potatoes close together in a baking dish. Fill the bottom of the dish with water and add the oil.
6. Cover the dish and steam in a hot oven for 20 minutes.
7. Before serving, top with sour cream and garnish with dill or parsley.

5. Potatoes with Sausages and Onions

Ingredients:
8 potatoes
15oz. cooked sausages
2 large onions
4 Tbsp. melted shortening, margarine, or butter
Salt
Pepper.

Preparation:
1. Peel the potatoes and cut them into small rounds. If you like, cut the sausages into chunks.
2. Cut the onions into rounds.
3. Combine the potatoes, sausages, and onions with the shortening, margarine, or butter in a pan.
4. Add salt and pepper to taste, cover the pan, and steam on low heat until the potatoes are soft.

6. French Potato

Ingredients:
1 1/2 lb. bacon
2 onions, chopped
1clove garlic, minced
1 tsp. each cumin, salt, and black or white pepper
10 potatoes
1/2 c. sour cream

Preparation:
1. Cut the bacon into small slices and sauté with the onions.
2. Add the garlic, cumin, salt, and pepper.
3. Peel the potatoes and cut into small chunks. Place them in a pan, salt them, and cover them with sour cream.
4. Cover and steam on low heat until the potatoes are soft. Top with the bacon mixture and serve.

7. Hungarian Potato

Ingredients:
10 potatoes
2 onions
1/2 tsp. ground red pepper
2 Tbsp. tomato paste
5 Tbsp. butter
1 c. beef stock
Salt
Fresh parsley or dill, chopped

Preparation:
1. Cut the potatoes into rounds. Thinly slice the onions and sauté with the potatoes.
2. Add the red pepper to the potatoes and onions and stir.
3. Add the onions and potatoes to a baking dish. Heat the beef stock and pour over the onions and potatoes. Cover the dish and steam in a hot oven until the potatoes are soft.
4. Before serving, cover with butter and garnish with dill or parsley.

8. Bacon with Potato Noodles

Ingredients:
10 potatoes
2 Tbsp. flour
2 eggs yolks
2 Tbsp. shortening
6 Tbsp. grated cheese (cheddar, Parmesan, or any cheese you like)
6-7oz. bacon, fried
1 tsp. salt
Pepper.

Preparation:
1. Peel the potatoes, boil them, and mash them.
2. Add flour, egg yolks, shortening, and salt and pepper to taste. Stir to combine.
3. Form the batter into noodles and cook in salted water.
4. Drain the noodles and add to a pan with the fried bacon. Add the cheese, stir, cover, and steam over low heat.

9. Steamed Potatoes

Ingredients:
6 potatoes
2 Tbsp. butter
1/2 tsp. salt

Preparation:
1. Peel the potatoes and put them into a large pot.
2. Fill a small dish halfway with water and place it in the center of the large pot, surrounded by the potatoes. Cover and cook in a hot oven until the potatoes are soft.
3. Serve topped with salt and melted butter.

4. Cooked Potatoes

1. Lemon-Butter Red Potatoes

Ingredients:
12 small red potatoes
1/3 c. butter
3 Tbsp. lemon juice
1 tsp. salt
1 tsp. grated lemon peel
1/4 tsp. pepper
1/8 tsp. ground nutmeg
2 Tbsp. minced fresh parsley

Preparation:
1. Peel the potatoes.
2. Add the potatoes to a large saucepan and cover with water.
3. Bring to a boil. Reduce heat, cover, and cook for 15 to 20 minutes or just until tender.
4. Meanwhile, in a small saucepan, melt the butter. Stir in lemon juice, salt, lemon peel, pepper, and nutmeg.
5. Drain the potatoes and place in a serving bowl.
6. Pour the butter mixture over the potatoes and toss gently to coat. Garnish with parsley.

2. Diet Potato

Ingredients:
2 carrots
6oz. celery
12oz. cauliflower
3 Tbsp. olive oil
1 small bunch green parsley, minced
1/2 tsp. salt
8 potatoes
1 c. vegetable stock
1 c. tomato juice

Preparation:
1. Peel the carrots and chop all the vegetables into small pieces.
2. Toss with oil, parsley, and salt, and steam.
3. Peel and rinse the potatoes. Scoop out the insides with a spoon.
4. Place the potatoes in a pan and fill them with the vegetable mixture. Pour the stock over the top, cover, and cook until the potatoes are almost tender.
5. Add the tomato juice and cook for several minutes.

3. Potato Sausages

Ingredients:
6 potatoes
2 Tbsp. flour
½ tsp. salt, pepper

For the sauce:
1 onion, finely diced
1 Tbsp. shortening
2 Tbsp. tomato paste
1 Tbsp. cheddar cheese

Preparation:
1. Boil the potatoes in their skins, then peel them, and then grate them or mash them.
2. Add flour, salt, and pepper and stir until the mixture forms a tight dough.
3. Form the dough into small sausages and boil in salted water.
4. To make the sauce, sauté the onion in shortening. Add the tomato paste and a small amount of water and cook until the onion is soften.
5. Top the hot sausages with sauce and cheese.

4. Stuffed Baby Red Potatoes

Ingredients:
24 small red potatoes
1/4 c. butter, cubed
1/2 c. shredded Parmesan cheese, divided
1/2 c. crumbled cooked bacon, divided
2/3 c. sour cream,
1 egg, beaten,
1/2 tsp. salt
1/8 tsp. pepper
1/8 tsp. paprika

Preparation:
1. Scrub the potatoes, place them in a large saucepan, and cover them with water.
2. Bring to a boil. Reduce the heat, cover, and cook for 15 to 20 minutes or until tender. Drain.
3. When the potatoes are cool enough to handle, cut a thin slice off the top of each potato. Scoop out the pulp, leaving a thin shell. (Cut thin slices from the bottoms of the potatoes to level them, if necessary.)

4. In a large bowl, mash the potato tops and pulp with butter. Set aside 2 tablespoons each of the Parmesan cheese and bacon for the garnish; add the remaining cheese and bacon to the potatoes.
5. Stir in the sour cream, egg, salt, and pepper. Spoon the mixture into the potato shells. Top with the remaining cheese and bacon. Sprinkle with paprika.
6. Place in an ungreased 15 × 10 inch baking pan. Bake at 375°F for 12 to 18 minutes.

5. Potato Noodles

Ingredients:
6 large potatoes
6 oz. butter
3 eggs, separated
1/2 tsp. salt
4-5 Tbsp. flour

Preparation:
1. Boil the potatoes in their skins. Peel them and grate them.
2. Fold the butter with the potatoes. Add the egg yolks, salt, and flour. Stir until the mixture forms hard dough.
3. Beat the egg whites until medium or stiff peaks and add them to the dough.
4. Form the dough into round noodles and boil in salted water.
5. Drain the noodles. Serve topped with melted butter, sauce, or mushrooms and garnish with herb.

6. Rough Noodles

Ingredients:
8 potatoes
1/2 c. milk
17oz. fresh mushrooms, chopped finely
2 Tbsp. butter
1 small bunch parsley, minced
1 tsp. salt
2 Tbsp. grated cheddar cheese

Preparation:
1. Peel and boil the potato. Grate and rinse them. Put the grated potatoes in a bowl and cover with hot milk.
2. Sauté the mushrooms with butter.
3. Add the mushrooms, minced parsley, and salt to the potatoes and stir until the mixture forms the nice dough.
4. Form the dough into small shaped noodles; then boil them in salted water.
5. Drain the noodles and serve topped with cheese.

7. Meat-Filled Dumplings

Ingredients
10 potatoes
3/4 c. flour
1 Tbsp. potato starch or flour
2 whole eggs

For the filling:
300 g ground beef
1 onion, chopped
1 Tbsp. butter
Pepper
Salt

Preparation:
1. Boil the potatoes and mash them. Add the flour and eggs and combine thoroughly into the dough.
2. To prepare the filling, sauté the beef in butter with onion, black pepper, and salt.
3. Form the dough into round dumplings. Push the meat filling inside the dumplings.
4. Put the dumplings in boiling water and cook until soft and floating in the water.
5. Remove the dumplings from the water and serve hot with butter, sauce, or fried bacon.

8. TRIANGLES

Ingredients:
8 potatoes
1/2 c. flour
1/2 c. potato flour or starch
2 eggs
Nutmeg finely grounded, salt, pepper
2 Tbsp. bread crumbs
2 Tbsp. butter

For the filling:
3oz. dried mushrooms
1 onion, minced
1 Tbsp. butter

Preparation:
1. Boil the potatoes, drain the water, and mash. Allow to cool.
2. To the cooled potatoes, add the flour, potato flour, and eggs. Mix thoroughly.
3. Turn out the dough onto a lightly floured board and roll out until the dough is 0.5 centimeter thick (or a little less than 1/4 inch). Cut into squares.
4. To prepare the filling, rehydrate the mushrooms by soaking them in hot water. When wet sauté the mushrooms with the onions in butter.
5. Place a small portion of mushroom filling in the center of each square. Fold the dough over the filling to form a triangle and press the sides closed.
6. Simmer the triangles in salted water on low heat for 20 minutes. Remove the triangles from the water. Serve covered with bread crumbs and butter.

9. Grated German Noodles

Ingredients:
1/2 loaf French bread
4 large potatoes
1/2 tsp. salt
1/2 gal milk
1 c. barley
2 Tbsp. butter

Preparation:
1. Cut the bread into small cubes and toast in a pan until golden.
2. Peel and boil the potatoes. When cooled, grate them and add salt.
3. Bring the milk to a boil and add barley. Stir in the grated potatoes. Mix thoroughly to form light dough.
4. Bring a pot of salted water to a boil.
5. Forming noodles by rolling small amounts of potato-barley dough along with some of the bread into balls. To make the formation easier, keep your hands wet. Drop each ball into the boiling water.
6. When all the noodles have been added to the pot, reduce the heat to low and simmer for 20 minutes.

10. Garlic Mashed Potatoes

Ingredients:
2 1/4 lb. russet or Yukon Gold potatoes
1 whole garlic bulb
1 Tbsp. olive oil
1/2 c. sour cream
2 Tbsp. (1/4 stick) butter
1/8 tsp. salt
1/8 tsp. black pepper
1 small bunch fresh chives

Preparation:
1. Preheat the oven to 375°F. Peel the potatoes and cut into evenly sized pieces. Place in a large pot of lightly salted water. Bring to a boil and then reduce the heat and simmer until cooked through, about 20 minutes.
2. Meanwhile, separate garlic cloves but do not peel them. Place them in a bowl, add olive oil, and toss to coat. Place on a baking sheet and roast in the oven until softened, about 10 minutes.
   Allow to cool slightly.
3. Drain the potatoes and return them to the pot. Mash slightly. Add sour cream and butter. Quickly squeeze the pulp from the garlic cloves into the pot. Add salt and black pepper.
4. Mash the potatoes until combined and smooth. Transfer to a serving bowl. Cut the chives into small pieces and sprinkle them over the mashed potatoes for garnish.

11. Creamed Potato and Peas

Ingredients:
1 lb. small red potatoes
2 1/2 c. frozen peas
1/4 c. butter, cubed
1 green onion, sliced
1/4 c. flour
1/2 teaspoon salt
1 dash pepper
2 c. milk

Preparation:
1. Scrub and quarter the red potatoes. Place them in a large saucepan and cover with water.
2. Bring to a boil. Reduce the heat, cover, and simmer for 10 minutes. Add the peas and cook 5 minutes longer or until the potatoes and peas are tender.
3. Meanwhile, in another large saucepan, melt the butter. Add onion and sauté until tender. Stir in the flour, salt, and pepper until blended. Gradually add the milk. Bring to a boil. Cook and stir for 1 to 2 minutes or until thickened. Drain the potatoes and peas and combine with the sauce.

12. Colorful Potato Puree

Ingredients:
10 potatoes
2 Tbsp. butter
1 c. milk
9oz. spinach
1 egg yolk
2 Tbsp. tomato paste
Salt to the taste.

Preparation:
1. Peel the potatoes and boil for several minutes. When cooked through, drain the potatoes.
2. Mashed the potatoes and add butter and hot milk.
3. Blend the potatoes in a blender until soft and creamy.
4. Separate into 3 parts. Mix spinach into the first, tomato paste into the second, and egg yolk into the third.

13. Onion Puree

Ingredients:
6 potatoes
4 large onions
1 c. milk
2 Tbsp. butter
3 egg yolks
1 dash nutmeg
1/2 tsp. salt
1/2 tsp. pepper

Preparation:
1. Peel the potatoes and the onions. Cook them together in small amount of water.
2. Drain the vegetables and grate them.
3. Add the grated vegetables to the bowl of an electric mixer. Add hot milk, butter, and egg yolks. Beat with the mixer until smooth.
4. Add the nutmeg, salt, and pepper. Serve garnished with dill or parsley.

5. FRIED POTATOES

1. Chili-Style Potatoes

Ingredients:
10 potatoes
1 c. milk
1 to 2 eggs
12oz. ground beef
Salt
Pepper
3 Tbsp. flour
4 Tbsp. shortening

Preparation:
1. Peel the potatoes and boil them in salted water.
2. Drain the water, mash the potatoes, and add hot milk. Let cool.
3. Add the eggs and combine thoroughly into fine dough.
4. Roll out the dough and cut into squares. Spoon the ground beef (either cooked or raw and seasoned with salt and pepper) into the center of each square.
5. Fold the dough over the filling and seal the sides to form small dumplings (pierogies). Dredge with flour and fry in hot shortening.

2. Potato Cutlets

Ingredients:
10 potatoes
3 eggs
2 tsp. sugar
2 Tbsp. butter
1/2 tsp. salt
4 to 5 Tbsp. bread crumbs
2 to 3 Tbsp. shortening

Preparation:
1. Peel the potatoes and boil until soft.
2. Stir in 2 eggs, sugar, butter, and salt.
3. Form the potatoes into cutlets. Beat the remaining egg. Dredge the cutlets in the egg and then in the bread crumbs. On the warmed pan Stir-fry in the shortening until golden.

3. Potato Cutlets with Apples

Ingredients:
10 potatoes
2 Tbsp. melted butter
2 eggs, separated
2 large apples
1/2 tsp. baking soda
2 Tbsp. flour
1/2 tsp. sea salt.
2 to 3 Tbsp. bread crumbs
2 to 3 Tbsp. shortening

Preparation:
1. Boil the potatoes in their skin. When they've cooled enough
    to handle, peel them and mash them in an electric mixer until
    smooth.
2. In a small bowl, whisk the butter with the egg yolks.
3. Peel the apples and grate on the large holes of a box grater.
4. Beat the egg whites until stiff peaks form and add the baking
    soda, when ready
5. Thoroughly combine all the previous ingredients, adding salt
    and flour.
6. Form the dough into cutlets. Dredge in bread crumbs and pan
    fry in hot shortening.

4. Potato Cutlets with Nuts

Ingredients:
5 potatoes
1 medium onion, minced
1 Tbsp. butter
6oz. chopped walnuts
3 eggs
2 tsp. dill, chopped
4 Tbsp. bread crumbs
2 Tbsp. flour
2 Tbsp. butter, margarine, or shortening for frying.

Preparation:
1. Peel the potatoes and boil in salted water until soft. Drain the water and mash.
2. Sauté the onion in 1 tablespoon butter.
3. Blend the potatoes and onion with nuts, 2 eggs, dill, and half of the bread crumbs.
4. Beat the remaining egg and combine the remaining bread crumbs with the flour.
5. Form the mixture into cutlets. Dredge in the beaten egg and then in the bread crumbs with flour.
6. Pan fry the cutlets in hot butter, margarine, or shortening.

5. Potato Croquettes

Ingredients:
10 potatoes
2 eggs
1/2 tsp. each salt and pepper
12oz. cooked ground beef
1 Tbsp. bread crumbs
2 to 3 Tbsp. shortening for frying

Preparation:
1. Peel the potatoes and boil until soft. Drain the water and grind with a mill.
2. Combine 1 egg, salt, pepper, and beef with the potatoes.
3. If the batter is very thin, add some flour.
4. Beat the remaining egg.
5. Roll the dough into small balls. Dredge the balls in the beaten egg and then in the bread crumbs.
6. Drop the balls into hot shortening and fry.

6. Potato Pretzels

Ingredients:
14 potatoes
2 eggs
1 Tbsp. butter
1 Tbsp. sour cream
1 dash minced nutmeg
½ tsp. salt
1 c. olive oil
1 Tbsp. butter
2 to 3 Tbsp. bread crumbs.

Preparation:
1. Peel the potatoes, boil, and then cool and grate.
2. Add eggs, butter, sour cream, nutmeg, and salt.
3. Blend all ingredients into fine dough.
4. Form the dough into pretzels and pan fry in the oil.

7. Potato Pancakes

Ingredients:
7 potatoes
1 c. all-purpose flour
15 g yeast
1 c. milk
½ tsp. salt
2 Tbsp. potato flour
2 eggs
2 to 3 Tbsp. shortening for frying

Preparation:
1. Peel the potatoes, grate, and then rinse and drain thoroughly.
2. Combine the potatoes with all-purpose flour, yeast, and warm milk.
3. Add salt to the yeast mixture, mix, and let rise in a pot for 30 minutes.
4. Mix the potato flour and eggs into the yeast and let rise for 1 hour.
5. When the dough is ready form it into pancakes, and pan fry in hot shortening.

8. Potato Nuts

Ingredients:
10 potatoes
1/2 c. flour
2 eggs
1/2 c. sour cream
1 tsp. pepper
1/2 tsp. salt
2 to 3 Tbsp. shortening for frying
fresh green herbs for garnish

Preparation:
1. Boil the potatoes in their skins; then peel and grind with a mill.
2. Mix in the rest of the ingredients and refrigerate for 20 minutes.
3. Form the dough into balls, dredge them in flour, and pan fry them in the hot shortening.
4. Garnish with fresh dill, parsley, or other green herbs.

9. Potato Doughnuts, Savory

Ingredients:
7 potatoes
1/2oz. yeast
2 Tbsp. sour cream or heavy cream
2 eggs
Dash black pepper
1/2 tsp. salt
2 to 3 Tbsp. shortening for frying

Preparation:
1. Boil the potatoes in their skins; then peel and grind with a mill. Allow to cool.
2. To the cooled potatoes, add yeast, cream, eggs, salt, and pepper.
3. Blend the ingredients thoroughly. Form the dough into balls and fry in hot shortening.
4. Drain on paper towels and serve warm.

10. Potato Pancake Variations

Ingredients:
10 potatoes
2 to 3 Tbsp. flour
1/2 tsp. salt
Small dash black pepper
1 tsp. Vegeta (dried vegetable seasoning)
3 eggs, beaten
3 Tbsp. oil for frying

Preparation:
1. Peel the potatoes and grate on the large holes of a box grater.
2. Mix the flour, salt, pepper, Vegeta, and beaten eggs with the potatoes.
3. In a small pan (the size of a dessert plate), heat the oil.
4. Pour 1/3 to 1/2 inch of batter into the pan.
5. Fry until lightly golden on both sides. Serve hot covered with spicy meat sauce.

For a variation, add sharp cheddar cheese and bread crumbs instead of flour.

11. Potato Cheese Pancakes

Ingredients:
5 large potatoes
17oz. cottage cheese
Just less than 1 c. flour
1 egg
1/2 tsp. salt
2 to 3 Tbsp. oil for frying.

Preparation:
1. Peel the potatoes and boil until soft.
2. Drain the potatoes, mash them, and let cool.
3. Add cheese, flour, egg, and salt to the potatoes and mix thoroughly. Form round cakes and pan fry in oil until both sides are brown.

12. Potato Pancakes with Garlic Sauce

Ingredients:
10 to 15 small potatoes
7 to 8 Tbsp. sunflower oil

For the sauce:
5 garlic cloves,
2 Tbsp. sunflower oil or olive oil.

Preparation:
1. Peel and slice the potatoes. Dry on paper towels.
2. Heat the oil in a pan and fry the potato slices.
3. Meanwhile, to make the sauce, combine the garlic and oil.
4. Remove the potatoes from oil and top with garlic sauce.

6. Baked Potatoes

1. Potato Cake with Bacon

Ingredients:
15oz. lightly striped bacon, or 50 g whole bacon
1 onion, chopped
10 large potatoes
1 egg, beaten
1 Tbsp. bread crumbs
Salt
Pepper

Preparation:
1. Preheat the oven to 350 °F
2. Cut the bacon into small pieces and sauté until crisp. Sauté the onion. Crumble a small amount of the bacon and set aside.
2. Grate the uncooked potatoes. Add small cut bacon fried with onion and egg beaten, pepper, salt.
3. Grease a pan with shortening and dust it with bread crumbs.
4. Pour the potato batter into the pan, sprinkle flakes of bacon on top, and bake for 1 hour, or until golden and the sides pull away from the pan.
5. Cut with knife into pieces.
6. Serve with sour cream or meat sauce.

Tips: The cake can be prepared without bacon by adding 1 additional egg.
To remove the cake from the pan easily, lay a cloth soaked with cold water under the pan.

2. Potato Rolls

Ingredients:
10 large potatoes
½ tsp. salt
½ tsp. pepper
1 onion
6oz. lard
1/2 c. sour cream

Preparation:
1. Preheat the oven to 350°F
2. Grate half of the potatoes and rinse. Squeeze excess water from the potatoes through a cheesecloth.
3. Boil the other half of the potatoes; then mash and combine with the grated potato, pepper, and salt.
4. Stir until a dough forms. Form the dough into rolls 2 to 3 inches in diameter and cut them into slices.
5. Put the roll slices onto a baking sheet and bake for 45-50 minutes or until gold and soft.
6. Brush the rolls with shortening and top with fried onion and with sour cream.
7. Serve hot.

3. Potato Cake

Ingredients:
10 potatoes
1 egg
1/4 tsp. each off : grounded nutmeg, salt, and pepper
7 Tbsp. grated cheese
3/4 c. milk
2 to 3 cloves garlic, minced
3 Tbsp. butter

Preparation:
1. Preheat the oven to 330-345 °F
2. Peel the potatoes and slice thinly. Place them in a large bowl.
3. Add the egg, nutmeg, salt, pepper, nutmeg, half the cheese, and milk to the potatoes. Mix all ingredients thoroughly.
4. Grease a deep casserole dish with butter and add the garlic at the bottom.
5. Pour the potato mixture into the dish.
6. Sprinkle the top with the remaining grated cheese and pats of butter.
7. Bake 40 minutes.

4. Round Potato Cake

Ingredients:
12 large potatoes
2 onions
2 to 3 egg whites
1 tsp. Vegeta (dried vegetable seasoning)
1/2 tsp. salt
1/2 tsp. pepper
2/3 c. flour
4 Tbsp. shortening

Preparation:
1. Preheat the oven to 335-345 °F
2. Peel and grate the potatoes and the onions.
3. Whisk the egg whites until stiff peaks form.
4. Fold the potatoes and onions into the egg whites. Add the Vegeta, salt, pepper, and flour. The dough should be light and fluffy.
5. Grease a deep casserole dish with butter.
6. Pour the batter into the dish. Sprinkle shortening flakes on top and bake for 1 hour or until light brown.
7. When hot, cut into squares and serve with spicy meat sauce and cooked sour cabbage.

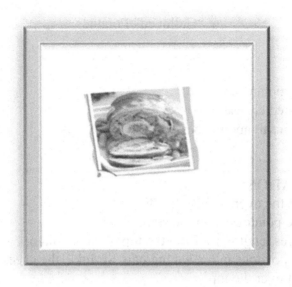

5. Onion Potato Cake

Ingredients:
6 to 8 large potatoes
4 onions
1 tsp. Vegeta,
1/2 tsp. salt
1/2 tsp. pepper
Several slices smoked bacon (for lining the pan)
2 to 3 Tbsp. shortening (for greasing the pan)
1 Tbsp. lard

Preparation:
1. Preheat the oven to 335-345 °F
2. Grate the potatoes with the large holes of a box grater. Grate the onions in the same way.
3. Add the Vegeta, salt, and pepper, and thoroughly mix.
4. Grease a casserole dish and line the bottom with bacon slices.
5. Pour the potato-onion mixture into the pan. Sprinkle lard flakes over the top.
6. Bake for 50-75 min until soft and golden.

6. "Galloped" Potatoes

Ingredients:
10 medium potatoes
3 Tbsp. grated cheese
1/2 tsp. each salt and pepper
9oz. butter

PREPPARATION:
1. Preheat the oven to 320-335°F
2. Peel the potatoes from the skin.
3. Cut slices lengthwise from the top of each potato.
4. Put the potatoes into a baking pan. Sprinkle the cheese, pepper, and salt over the top.
5. Put a small piece of butter on each potato.
6. Bake 45 min or until golden.

7. Baked Potato with Mushrooms

Ingredients:
8 potatoes
4 eggs
17oz. fresh mushrooms
1 onion, chopped
3 Tbsp. flour
2 Tbsp. butter (plus more for greasing the pan)
2 Tbsp. bread crumbs
1/2 c. sour cream
1/2 tsp. salt
1/2 tsp. pepper
Parsley, dill, or other herbs you like, chopped

Preparation.
1. Preheat the oven to 330 °F
2. Boil the potatoes in their skins. When they're soft and cool enough to handle, peel and slice them into squares.
3. Hard-boil 3 of the eggs. When they've cooled enough to handle, peel them and slice them thinly.
4. Boil the mushrooms just until soft. Slice thinly. Set some aside for layering on top of the casserole. Sauté the rest with the onion in butter.
5. Add the flour and sour cream to the mushrooms and onions. Stir until incorporated.
6. Grease a casserole dish with butter and dust it with bread crumbs.
   Place half the potatoes into the baking dish. On top, layer the eggs, mushroom-onion mixture, and fresh herbs, and then the other half of the potatoes.
7. Top the potatoes with the reserved sliced mushrooms, salt, and pepper. Brush the top with a beaten egg.
8. Bake 30 minutes or until light brown.

8. Baked Potato with Apples and Rice

Ingredients:
10 potatoes, diced finely
15oz. apples, cored and sliced thinly
1 onion, minced
3 Tbsp. butter (plus extra for greasing the pan)
1/2 c. rice
1 egg, beaten
Salt to taste
2 Tbsp. bread crumbs

Preparation:
1. Preheat the oven to 345 °F
2. Sauté the potatoes, apples, and onion in half the butter.
3. Cook the rice according to the package directions. When soft, stir in the potatoes, apples, onion, and egg. Add salt to taste.
4. Grease an oven-safe frying pan with butter and dust with bread crumbs.
5. Pour the mixture into the pan and bake for 30 minutes.

9. Mother in Love Baked Potatoes

Ingredients:
12 potatoes
2/3 c. flour
1 egg
1/2 tsp. salt
1 tsp. baking soda
9oz. lard
5 to 6 garlic cloves, minced

Preparation:
1. Preheat the oven to 340°F
2. Peel the potatoes, boil them until soft, and mash them.
3. To the potatoes, add the flour, egg, salt, and baking soda and mix.
4. Form the dough into rolls 1 inch in diameter.
5. Bake the rolls on a greased baking sheet until golden.
6. Meanwhile, sauté the garlic in the lard with a pinch of salt.
7. When the rolls are done, transfer them to a large pot and cover with the sautéed garlic.
8. Cover the pan and cook until rolls are soft, stirring several times.

Variation: Use 1 to 2 tablespoons yeast bloomed in warm milk instead of the baking soda for softer rolls.

10. Baked Potatoes with Tomatoes

Ingredients:
10 potatoes
4 large tomatoes
4 onions, finely diced
4 Tbsp. butter
Oil shortening (for greasing the pan)
1/2 c. sour cream
1/2 tsp. pepper
1/2 tsp. salt
1 bunch fresh parsley, minced

Preparation:
1. Preheat the oven to 335°F
2. Boil the potatoes in their skins. When cool enough to handle, slice them.
3. Soak the tomatoes in hot water and remove the skins.
4. Sauté the onions and tomatoes in butter.
5. Grease a baking dish with shortening. In the dish, layer half the potatoes, the tomato-onion mixture, and then the rest of the potatoes.
6. Add the salt and pepper to the sour cream and pour over the top of the potatoes.
7. Bake for 30 minutes.
8. Before serving, sprinkle with parsley on top.

11. Baked Potatoes Savoy

Ingredients:
6 potatoes
1 c. milk
2 eggs
3 Tbsp. sharp cheddar cheese
1 dash nutmeg, grated
1/2 tsp. pepper
1/2 tsp. salt
shortening (for greasing the baking dish)

Preparation;
1. Preheat the oven to 345 °F
2. Peel the potatoes and slice them thinly.
3. Whip the eggs with the milk.
4. Add half the cheese and all of the nutmeg, pepper, and salt.
5. In a baking dish greased with shortening, spread the potato slices. Pour the milk and cheese mixture over the top.
6. Sprinkle the rest of the cheese on top and bake for 50 minutes.

12. Baked Potatoes with Cheese

Ingredients:
12 small potatoes
12 oz. sharp cheddar cheese
1/2 tsp. pepper
1/2 tsp. salt,
2 Tbsp. shortening (for greasing the pan)
3 Tbsp. butter

Preparation:
1. Preheat the oven to 320-330 °F
2. Peel the potatoes and cut a slice lengthwise from the bottom of each one so they stand steady.
3. Cut a slight lengthwise down the middle of each potato, but do not break them apart.
4. Cut the cheese into sticks and place the sticks in the slits of the potatoes.
5. Set the potatoes in a greased baking dish. Sprinkle salt and pepper on top and cover with butter.
6. Bake for 45 minutes.

13. Sausage-Potato Supper

Ingredients:
2 small red potatoes, cubed
1 small zucchini, cut into 1/4-in. slices
1/4 to 1/2 tsp. garlic salt
1 Tbsp. butter
1/2 lb. smoked sausage, cut into 1/2-in. slices
4 Tbsp. grated Parmesan cheese, divided
1/8 to 1/4 tsp. pepper

Preparation:
1. Place the potatoes in a small saucepan and cover with water. Bring to a boil. Reduce the heat, cover, and cook for 15 minutes or until tender.
2. Meanwhile, sprinkle garlic salt over the zucchini. In a small skillet, sauté the zucchini in butter until just tender. Add the sausage and cook until browned.
3. Drain the potatoes and add them to the skillet. Sprinkle with 2tablespoons of the Parmesan and the pepper and heat through. Top with the remaining cheese.

14. Potato Straws with Meat

Ingredients:
15oz. meat, ground
Vegetables that you like, such as carrot, parsley, dill, and corn
1 large onion, chopped
2 Tbsp. butter
8 potatoes
Salt to taste
1/2 Tbsp. flour
2 c. beef bouillon
1 Tbsp. bread crumbs
3 Tbsp. grated cheddar or gouda cheese

Preparation:
1. Preheat the oven to 330 °F
2. Cook the meat with the vegetables until the meat is well done and the vegetables are soft.
3. Sauté the onion in butter and add it to the meat and vegetables.
4. Peel the potatoes, cut them into straws, and stir into the meat and vegetables. Add salt to taste.
5. Spread the potatoes and meat in a baking dish. Sprinkle with flour and pour the bouillon over the top.
6. Sprinkle cheese and bread crumbs over the top and bake about 45 minutes.

15. Salted Fingers

Ingredients:
6 potatoes
6 to 8 Tbsp. cottage cheese or farmer's cheese
15oz. butter
1/2 tsp. salt
2 to 3 c. flour
1/2 tsp. baking soda
2 egg whites
1 tsp. cumin

Preparation:
1. Preheat the oven to 350°F
2. Peel and grate the potatoes.
3. Add the cheese, butter, salt, flour, and baking soda and blend together to make fine dough.
4. Form the dough into skinny rolls 1 to 3 inches long and place on a baking sheet.
5. Brush each roll with egg whites and sprinkle with cumin.
6. Bake until golden.

16. Individual Soufflés

Ingredients:
9 potatoes
4 eggs, separated
4 Tbsp. grated cheese
4 Tbsp. butter, plus more for greasing the ramekins
Salt to taste
1/2 c. heavy cream
1 Tbsp. flour
4-5 Tbsp. cheddar cheese, grated
3 Tbsp. butter, melted

Preparation:
1. Preheat the oven to 345°F
2. Peel the potatoes and boil until soft. Drain them and mash them.
3. Add the egg yolks, cheese, butter, and salt. Mix thoroughly.
4. Whip the egg whites with the heavy cream. Fold into the potatoes.
5. Grease small ramekins with butter and dust with flour.
6. Pour the batter into the ramekins. Sprinkle cheese and drizzle melted butter on top of each one.
7. Bake for 60 min until soft and gold.

17. Potato Filled with Bacon

Ingredients:
10 potatoes
9oz. bacon
2 Tbsp. butter (for greasing the baking sheet)
1/2 tsp. each salt and pepper.

Preparation:
1. Preheat the oven to 350°F
2. Peel the potatoes and sprinkle with salt.
3. With a paring knife, cut a hole in the center of each potato. Do not cut all the way through.
4. In each hole, place 1 rolled-up strip of bacon.
5. Place the potatoes onto a baking sheet and bake for 45 minutes.

18. Potato with Tuna Fish

Ingredients:
8 to 10 potatoes
2 tuna steaks
2 onions, chopped
2 Tbsp. butter, plus more for greasing a baking sheet
1 tsp. salt
2 Tbsp. bread crumbs
1/2 c. heavy cream

Preparation:
1. Preheat the oven to 350°F
2. Peel the potatoes and boil just until soft. When cool enough to handle, cut into thin squares.
3. Soak the tuna, then drain it, and cut it into small chunks.
4. Sauté the onion in butter.
5. Grease a baking sheet with butter.
6. Place the potatoes on the baking sheet and layer each potato with tuna and onion. Sprinkle bread crumbs and drizzle heavy cream over the top.
7. Bake about 50 minutes.

19. Favorite Potatoes

Ingredients:
12 medium potatoes
3 Tbsp. walnuts, minced
4 Tbsp. bread crumbs
4 Tbsp. grated sharp cheddar cheese
1 tsp. Vegeta
Salt to taste
4 Tbsp. olive oil

Preparation:
1. Preheat the oven to 345°F
2. Peel the potatoes.
3. Cut a slice from the bottom of each potato to steady them on a baking sheet.
4. In a large bowl, combine the walnuts, bread crumbs, cheese, Vegeta, and salt.
5. Dredge each potato in olive oil and then in the bread crumb mixture.
6. Place on a baking sheet and bake for 45 minutes.

20. Potato-Bar Chili

Ingredients:
4 to 6 freshly baked potatoes
1 1/2 lbs. ground beef
2 medium onions, chopped
1 medium green pepper, chopped
One 28 oz. can diced tomatoes, undrained
One 15 1/2 oz. can chili beans, undrained
2 Tbsp. sugar
2 tsp. chili powder
1/4 tsp. salt
1/4 tsp. pepper

Preparation:
1. Slice the baked potatoes lengthwise down the middle. Do not cut through the potatoes.
2. In a Dutch oven, cook the beef, onions, and green pepper over medium heat until the meat is no longer pink. Drain.
3. Add the tomatoes, beans, sugar, and seasonings to the Dutch oven.
4. Bring to a boil. Reduce the heat and simmer, uncovered, for 20 minutes. Serve along with the beef mixture over baked potatoes.

21. Easy Topping Combinations for Baked Potatoes

1. Steamed veggies with yogurt or cottage cheese
2. Caramelized onions with shredded cheddar cheese
3. Olive oil, feta cheese, black olives, tomatoes, and basil
4. Gruyère cheese, sage, walnuts, and butter
5. Butter, garlic, parsley, chives, oregano, rosemary, and thyme
6. Cream cheese, basil, and spinach
7. Sour cream, tomato, onion, shredded Monterey Jack cheese, and cayenne pepper
8. Rosemary, Greek olives, Parmesan cheese, and tomatoes

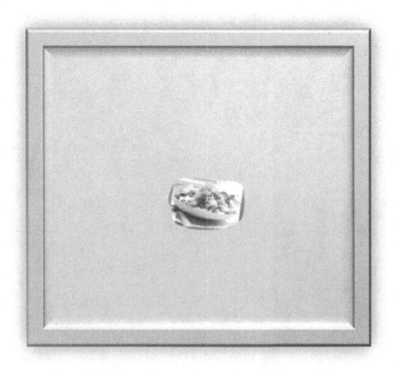

7. Sweet Potatoes

1. Grandmother's Potato Cake

Ingredients:
2 to 3 eggs, separated
6 potatoes,
1 Tbsp. butter,
Salt to taste
5 Tbsp. flour,
3oz. raisins
1 Tbsp. oil (for greasing the pan)
2 Tbsp. bread crumbs
1 Tbsp. fruit syrup

Preparation:
1. Preheat the oven to 345 °F
2. Whisk the egg whites to stiff peaks.
3. Peel and grate the potatoes. Combine with butter, salt, egg yolks, flour, and raisins.
4. Gently fold in the egg whites.
5. Grease a pan with the oil and dust with bread crumbs. Pour the batter into the pan.
6. Place the pan on the middle rack of the oven. Place a sheet pan with sides filled with water on the lower rack. Bake for 90 minutes.
7. Allow the cake to cool completely. Serve covered with fruit syrup.

2. Potato Cakes with Baking Soda

Ingredients:
5 potatoes
2 eggs,
5 to 6 Tbsp. sugar
2 Tbsp. oil
125 g milled nuts
Zest of 1 lemon
1 tsp. baking soda
1/2 tsp. salt
1 Tbsp. cinnamon
1 c. all-purpose flour, divided
1 Tbsp. butter (for greasing the baking sheet)

Preparation:
1. Preheat the oven to 325 °F
2. Bake the potatoes in the oven until just tender (be sure to pierce the skin several times). When cool enough to handle, peel and grate them.
3. Whip the eggs with the sugar until fluffy.
4. Add the oil, potatoes, nuts, lemon zest, baking soda, salt, cinnamon, and 3/4 cup flour. Mix thoroughly until the batter forms fine dough.
5. Roll out the dough and cut into 1 1/2-inch rectangles.
6. Dredge the rectangles in the remaining flour and place on a greased baking sheet.
7. Bake the cakes until gold for 35-50 min.

3. Sweet Potatoes and Apples

Ingredients:
5 medium sweet potatoes
5 medium tart apples, peeled and thinly sliced
1/2 c. sugar
1 Tbsp. cornstarch
1 c. cold water
1 tsp. lemon juice
1/4 c. butter, cubed
1/4 tsp. ground cinnamon
1/8 tsp. salt

Preparation:
1. Place the sweet potatoes in a large pot and cover with water. Bring to a boil, reduce the heat, cover, and cook for 20 minutes or just until tender.
2. Drain the sweet potatoes and cool slightly. Peel and cut into 1/4-inch slices.
3. In a greased 13 × 9-inch baking dish, layer half of the apples and then half of the sweet potatoes. Repeat the layers.
4. In a small saucepan, combine the sugar, cornstarch, water, and lemon juice until smooth. Bring to a boil and cook, stirring, for 2 minutes or until thickened. Remove from the heat. Stir in the butter, cinnamon, and salt. Pour over the sweet potatoes and apples.
5. Cover the baking dish and bake at 350°F for 30 minutes. Uncover and bake for 10 more minutes or until the apples are tender.

4. Mini Potato Cakes

Ingredients:
4 potatoes
1 c. coffee
1 1/2 c. powdered sugar,
1 egg, beaten
15oz. sweet bread crumbs
1 orange peel, grated or sliced
7oz. grated nuts
1 1/2 oz. cacao
2 Tbsp. rum
4 Tbsp. coconut flakes

Preparation:
1. Boil the potatoes in their skins. Cool slightly and then peel and grate.
2. In a saucepan, cook the coffee with the sugar and egg. Allow to cool.
3. In a large bowl, combine the potatoes, bread crumbs, orange peel, nuts, cacao, rum, and coffee mixture. Mix thoroughly until the batter forms a stiff dough.
4. Form the batter into small balls. Dredge the balls in the coconut flakes, then serve cold or lightly warmed.

5. Apple Dumplings

Ingredients:
6 potatoes
1 egg
1/2 tsp. salt
1/2 c. flour
6 apples
1 Tbsp. lemon juice
1 Tbsp. butter, melted
1 1/2 to 2 c. milk
1 Tbsp. sugar

Preparation:
1. Boil the potatoes in their skins. Allow to cool slightly and then peel and mash.
2. Combine the potatoes with the egg, salt, and flour.
3. Stir thoroughly until the potato mixture forms fine dough. Roll out the dough and then cut into 24 squares.
4. Peel the apples, remove their cores, and cut each apple into quarters. Sprinkle with lemon juice.
5. Place 1 apple quarter onto each square of dough. Fold the dough over the apple and seal the edges.
6. Pour the butter into a baking dish and add the dumplings. Bake in a warm oven until the dough is golden.
7. Meanwhile, add sugar to the milk and stir until sugar is dissolved. Pour as much over the dumplings that they will absorb.
8. Continue baking the dumplings for several more minutes, until the apples are soft.
9. Pour the remaining milk over the dumplings just before serving.

6. Plum Dumplings

Ingredients:
6 potatoes
1/2 c. flour
1 egg
Salt to taste
6 medium plums
1 Tbsp. lemon juice
1 Tbsp. butter, melted
1 1/2 to 2 c. milk
1 dash sugar

Preparation:
1. Boil the potatoes in their skins. Allow to cool slightly and then peel and mash.
2. Fold the flour, egg, and salt into the potatoes.
3. Mix the batter thoroughly to form fine dough. Roll out the dough and cut into 24 squares.
4. Peel the plums, remove the pits, and cut into quarters. Sprinkle with lemon juice.
5. Place a plum quarter on each square of dough. Fold the dough over the plum and seal the edges.
6. Pour the butter into a baking dish and add the dumplings. Bake in a medium oven until the dough is golden.
7. Meanwhile, gradually add sugar to the milk. Stir until the sugar is dissolved. Pour as much over the dumplings as they will absorb.
8. Continue baking the dumplings until the plums are soft.
9. Pour the remaining milk over the dumplings just before serving.

7. Plum or Peach Dumplings

Ingredients:
6 potatoes
1 Tbsp. milk
1 Tbsp. sour cream
1 egg
1 egg yolk
1 tsp. butter
1 1/2 c. flour
1/2 box plums or peaches

Preparation;
1. Peel the potatoes and boil.
2. Mashed the potatoes and stir in the milk and sour cream. Then add the rest of the ingredients except the fruit and stir until the mixture forms a stiff dough.
3. Roll out the dough and cut into as many pieces as there are peaches or plums.
4. Remove the pits from the fruit. Put one whole peach or plum on each piece of dough. Stretch the dough to cover the fruit. Seal the edges.
5. Bring a pot of lightly salted water to a boil. Drop the dumplings into the water and cook until the fruit is soft.
6. Serve with melted butter.

8. Potato Balls with Plum Butter (Povidel).

Ingredients:
6 potatoes
1 egg, beaten
2 tsp. salt
1 Tbsp. butter
3 Tbsp. flour
3 Tbsp. plum butter (povidel)
½ cup olive oil, for frying
2 Tbsp. powdered sugar

Preparation:
1. Bake the potatoes; then peel and grind with a mill.
2. Blend the beaten egg, salt, butter, and flour into the potatoes. Stir until the mixture forms light dough.
3. Roll out the dough and cut into small pieces.
4. Put 1 to 2 teaspoons of povidel in the center of each piece of dough.
5. Fold the dough over the povidel and roll into a ball.
6. Drop the balls into hot oil and fry.
7. Drain the balls on paper towels. Sprinkle with powdered sugar.

9. Potato Legumina

Ingredients:
5 to 6 large potatoes
9oz. butter
2 whole eggs
2 eggs, separated
2 Tbsp. sugar
Fruit sauce or syrup of your choosing

Preparation:
1. Preheat the oven to 345°F
2. Boil the potatoes in their skins. Allow to cool slightly and then peel.
3. Mash the potatoes, adding the butter, whole eggs, and egg yolks
4. Add the sugar and continue mashing.
5. Beat the egg whites to stiff peaks. Fold into the potatoes.
6. Pour the batter into a baking pan and bake until golden.
7. Serve topped with fruit sauce or syrup.

10. Potato Doughnuts, Sweet

Ingredients:
6 potatoes
1 egg
1/2 tsp. salt
2 to 3 Tbsp. vanilla sugar
1 1/2 c. flour
2 oz. yeast
1 1/2 Tbsp. milk
2 Tbsp. sugar (for the yeast)
3 to 4 Tbsp. olive oil (for frying)
1/2 c. powdered sugar

Preparation:
1. Boil the potatoes in their skins. Allow to cool slightly; then peel and mash.
2. Stir the egg, salt, vanilla sugar, flour, and a small amount of the oil into the potatoes. Mix thoroughly.
3. Dissolve the sugar in warm milk. Stir in the yeast.
4. When the yeast foams, fold it into the potatoes to make a light batter. Allow the dough to rise for 1 hour covered with a towel.
5. Turn the dough out onto a floured board. Roll the dough to 1/2-inch thick.
6. Cut the dough into rounds with a small glass.
7. Fry the dough rounds in hot oil until golden.
8. Drain on paper towels and sprinkle with powdered sugar.

11. Potato Strudel

Ingredients:
6 potatoes
2 Tbsp. oil
4 Tbsp. sugar, divided
1 c. milk
50 g yeast
2 eggs
3 to 3 1/2 c. flour
Zest of 1 lemon
Salt to taste
1 1/2 to 2 kg apples
1 Tbsp. cinnamon
3/4 c. sugar
3 Tbsp. grated nuts
1 Tbsp. bread crumbs

Preparation:
1. Preheat the oven to 345°F
2. Boil the potatoes in their skins. All them to cool slightly and then peel, mash, or grate. Mix with oil.
3. Dissolve 2 tablespoons of sugar in warm milk and then stir in the yeast.
4. Beat the eggs with 2 tablespoons sugar.
5. Stir the flour yeast, eggs, lemon zest, and salt into the potatoes.
6. Stir the potatoes to form light dough. Allow the dough to rise.
7. Meanwhile, peel the apples and grate. In a pan over low heat, combine the cinnamon and 3/4 cup of sugar and stir. Keep warm.
8. Roll out the dough on a floured wooden board. Spread the nuts, bread crumbs, and apple mixture onto the dough. Sprinkle sugar over the top.
9. Roll the dough tightly into a log and sprinkle oil over the top.
10. Put the log on a baking sheet lined with parchment paper and bake for 45 minutes.

12. Tasty Potato Cake

Ingredients:
6 potatoes
2 to 3 eggs, separated
1 1/2 c. powdered sugar
1 to 2 drops lemon extract or the zest of an orange
1 1/2 tsp. cinnamon
1 Tbsp. baking soda
5 Tbsp. butter
3 c. flour
2 Tbsp. melted chocolate
2 tsp. vanilla sugar
3 Tbsp. ground nuts

Preparation:
1. Preheat the oven to 345°F
2. Boil the potatoes in their skins. After they've cooled slightly, peel and grind in a mill.
3. Whip the egg yolks with the powdered sugar to form a light batter; then fold into the potatoes.
4. Stir in the lemon extract or orange zest, cinnamon, baking soda, butter, and flour. Beat the egg whites to stiff peaks and gently fold them into the dough.
5. Grease a cake pan with butter, pour in the batter, and bake for 90 minutes.
6. After baking, transfer the cake to a dish and allow to cool. Top the cake with melted chocolate, vanilla sugar, and nuts.

13. Potato Cake with Cream Cheese

Ingredients:
5 potatoes
2 eggs, separated
3/4 c. sugar,
2 to 3 Tbsp. butter
16 oz. cream cheese
Zest of 1 orange
2 to 3 tsp. vanilla sugar
1 tsp. baking soda
12 oz. orange marmalade or any jam you like
2 to 3 Tbsp. powdered sugar

Preparation:
1. Preheat the oven to 345 °F
2. Boil the potatoes in their skins. When slightly cooled, peel and mash.
3. Whip the egg yolks, sugar, and butter into a light batter.
4. Add the cream cheese, orange zest, vanilla sugar, baking soda, mashed potatoes, and egg whites. Stir gently to combine all ingredients.
5. Transfer the dough into a greased baking pan and bake for 65 min.
6. Allow the cake to cool. Cut it into two layers and spread marmalade or jam on one layer. Stack the dry layer on top of the jam and powdered sugar over the top.

14. Sweet Potato Bread and Pineapple Butter

Ingredients:
1 3/4 c. flour
1 1/2 c. sugar
1 1/2 tsp. ground cinnamon
1 tsp. ground nutmeg
1/2 tsp. baking soda,
1/2 tsp. baking powder
1/2 tsp. salt
2 eggs
1 c. mashed sweet potatoes
1/2 c. canola oil
1/3 c. water

For the pineapple butter:
1/2 c. butter, softened
One 8 oz. can crushed pineapple, well drained

Preparation:

1. In a large bowl, combine the first seven ingredients (the flour through the salt).

2. In a small bowl, combine the eggs, sweet potatoes, oil, and water. Stir the mixture into the dry ingredients just until moistened.

3. Transfer to a greased 9 × 5-inch loaf pan. Bake at 350°F for 50 to 60 minutes or until a toothpick inserted near the center comes out clean.

4. Cool for 10 minutes before removing from the pan to a wire rack.

5. In a small bowl, combine the butter and pineapple. Serve with the bread.

15. Sweet Potato Waffles

Ingredients:
1 1/2 c. flour
1 Tbsp. sugar
1 1/2 tsp. baking powder
1 tsp. ground cardamom
1/2 tsp. salt
3 eggs, separated
1 c. sour cream
1 c. cold mashed sweet potatoes
1/2 c. milk
1/4 c. butter, melted
3/4 c. chopped pecans
maple syrup (optional)

Preparation:
1. In a large bowl, combine the flour, sugar, baking powder, cardamom, and salt.
2. In another bowl, whisk together the egg yolks, sour cream, sweet potatoes, milk, and butter. Stir into dry ingredients just until moistened. Fold in the pecans.
3. In a small bowl, beat the egg whites until stiff peaks form. Fold the egg whites into the batter.
4. Bake in a preheated waffle iron until golden brown. Serve topped with maple syrup.

8. POTATO SAUCES

1. Quick Hamburger Gravy

Ingredients:
1 1/2 lb. ground beef
2 medium onions, chopped
1/2 c. flour
2 Tbsp. beef bouillon granules
1/4 tsp. salt
1/4 tsp. pepper
5 c. milk
4 baked potatoes

Preparation:
1. In a Dutch oven, cook the ground beef and onions over medium heat until the meat is no longer pink. Drain.
2. Stir in the flour, beef bouillon granules, salt, and pepper.
3. Gradually add the milk and bring to a boil.
4. Cook and stir for 2 minutes or until thickened.
5. Serve over potatoes.

2. White Sauce

Ingredients:
2 Tbsp. butter
1 Tbsp. flour
1 1/2 c. beef or vegetable stock
1 egg yolk
Salt to taste

Preparation:
1. Over low heat, whisk together 1 tablespoon of the butter and the flour just until light brown.
2. Pour the cold stock into the pan and add the remaining butter.
3. Cook the stock on low heat for 5 minutes, stirring with a whisk.
4. Temper the egg yolk by whisking in a small amount of the sauce.
5. When the egg is warm, stir it into the cooked stock; then add salt.

3. Onion Sauce

Ingredients:
2 Tbsp. flour
2 Tbsp. butter
1 1/2 c. beef or vegetable stock
1/2 c. sour cream
1/2 tsp. salt
1 large onion, finely diced

Preparation:
1. Over low heat, whisk together the flour and butter just until light brown.
2. Whisk in the cold stock. Cook 15 to 20 minutes. Combine a small amount of warm stock with the sour cream. Add the mixture back to the sauce.
3. Cook on low heat about 5 minutes. Salt to the taste.
4. Meanwhile, sauté the onion in butter until golden brown. Stir into the sauce just before the sauce is done.

4. Mushroom Sauce

Ingredients:
3 oz. dried mushroom
1 Tbsp. flour
2 Tbsp. butter
1 onion, finely diced
1/2 tsp. salt

Preparation:
1. Clean the mushrooms with lukewarm water.
2. In a saucepan, soak the mushrooms 2 to 3 hours in the same water to reconstitute them, and then cook them over low heat. Remove the mushrooms, chop into small pieces, and set aside.
3. In a separate pan over low heat, whisk together the flour and butter until light brown. Pour the hot mushroom bouillon over the top and whisk until incorporated.
4. Continue cooking over low heat about 15 minutes.
5. Sauté the onion in butter until softened; then toss in the reserved mushrooms.
6. Add the onions and mushrooms to the sauce and heat. Add salt.

5. Tomato Sauce

Ingredients:
1 each parsley root, carrot, onion, finely diced
1 Tbsp. flour
1 and 1/2 c. heavy tomato sauce
1 c. beef stock
2 Tbsp. butter
1/2 tsp. each salt and pepper
Dash of crushed red pepper

Preparation:
1. Sauté the vegetables in butter until soft.
2. Add the flour and stir until lightly toasted. Combine the
   vegetables with the tomato sauce and stock in a saucepan.
3. Cook all ingredients on low heat for 10 minutes or until slightly
   reduced.
4. Stir in the butter and spices. Mix together and serve.

6. Regular Sauce

Ingredients:
1 Tbsp. flour
1 Tbsp. butter
1 c. beef or vegetable stock
3 Tbsp. scallions, minced
Salt and pepper

Preparation:
1. In a small saucepan, whisk together the butter and flour over low heat until light brown.
2. Pour in the stock and whisk to incorporate. Cook until warm.
3. Add the scallions and cook for several more minutes.
4. Add salt and pepper to taste.

7. Feast Sauce

Ingredients:
1 c. olive oil
1 Tbsp. flour
2 Tbsp. mustard
1 c. fish or vegetable stock
1/3 c. lemon juice
3 to 4 tsp. sugar
1/2 tsp. salt
1/2 c. cooked potatoes, cut into small chunks
1/2 c. carrots, chopped finely
1/2 c. fresh or frozen and thawed green peas

Preparation:
1. In a saucepan, whisk together the olive oil, flour, and mustard into a light batter.
2. Whisk in the bouillon and lemon juice, and then add salt and sugar.
3. Cook, stirring, over low heat, being careful not to overcook.
4. Before serving, stir in the vegetables.

8. Mustard Sauce

Ingredients:
1/4 c. sour cream
1 Tbsp. flour
2 egg yolks, cooked
3 Tbsp. mustard (or less, if desired)
Sugar, salt, and lemon juice to taste

Preparation:
1. In a saucepan, whisk together the sour cream and flour over low heat until warm.
2. In a separate bowl, thoroughly mix together the egg yolks, mustard, salt, sugar, and lemon juice.
3. Pour the egg mixture into the sour cream, stir, and heat on low heat.
4. Allow to cool. Serve on salads.

9. Light Red Sauce

Ingredients:
1 Tbsp. flour
2 Tbsp. butter, divided
1 Tbsp. tomato paste
2 c. beef stock
1 carrot, grated
1 parsley root, grated
2 Tbsp. white wine
1/2 tsp. each salt and pepper

Preparation:
1. In a saucepan over low heat, whisk together the flour and 1 tablespoon of butter.
2. Stir in the tomato paste and the stock.
3. Sauté the carrot and parsley root with the remaining tablespoon of butter until soft.
4. Combine the vegetables with wine, salt, and pepper. Stir into the stock and cook over low heat for 20 minutes.

10. Vanilla Sauce

Ingredients:
2 eggs, separated
1/2 c. milk
1/2 c. sugar
1 tsp. vanilla extract

Preparation:
1. Whisk the egg yolks with the sugar until the mixture is light yellow.
2. Heat the milk. Temper the egg yolks by whisking in a small amount of hot milk. When the yolks are warm, add them to the milk.
3. Add the vanilla and stir. If the sauce is too thin, cook over low heat, stirring, until reduced.

11. Sour Cream Sauce

Ingredients:
1 Tbsp. butter
1 Tbsp. potato flour
1 c. beef stock, heated
1/2 c. sour cream
1/2 tsp. each salt and pepper

Preparation:
1. In a small saucepan, melt the butter. Whisk in the flour and add hot stock.
2. Temper the sour cream by whisking in a small amount of the hot stock. When the sour cream is warm, stir it into the stock. Cook over low heat about 10 minutes.
3. Season with salt and pepper. If you like, add fresh dill or other herbs.

12. Sweet-and-Sour Sauce

Ingredients:
2 1/2 c. Light Red Sauce (see recipe 9 in this chapter)
2 to 3 Tbsp. tomato sauce
1 Tbsp. sugar
3 Tbsp. rye bread crumbs
1 small honey cookie, crumbled
1 Tbsp. lemon juice
1/2 c. orange marmalade
2 Tbsp. vinegar
1 Tbsp. diced pimientos
1/8 tsp. paprika
1 dash salt
other herbs you like, such as parsley, dill, scallions, oregano

Preparation:
1. In a saucepan, heat the Light Red Sauce. Stir in all the other ingredients.
2. Warm over low heat.

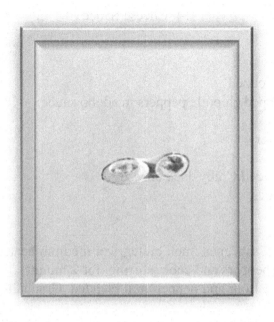

12. Delicious Sauce

Ingredients:
1 c. white wine
2 to 3 tsp. sugar
1 Tbsp. lemon juice,
1 1/2 c. beef stock, heated
5 Tbsp. bread crumbs
2 Tbsp. melted butter
salt to taste

Preparation:
1. In a saucepan, stir together the wine, sugar, lemon juice, and hot stock.
2. Add in the bread crumbs, butter, and salt and cook over low heat.
3. Before serving, strain the sauce through a sieve.

14. Cheese Sauce

Ingredients:
1/4 c. butter, cubed
2 Tbsp. chopped chipotle peppers in adobo sauce
1/4 c. flour
1/8 tsp. pepper
2 1/2 c. milk
1 1/2 c. shredded Colby-Jack cheese
Baked potatoes

Preparation:
1. In a small saucepan, melt butter over medium heat. Add chipotle peppers and cook, stirring, for 2 minutes.
2. Stir in the flour and pepper until blended. Gradually add the milk.
3. Bring to a boil. Cook, stir for 1 to 2 minutes or until thickened.
4. Stir in the cheese until melted.
5. Serve over potatoes.

15. Plum Sauce

Ingredients:
1/2 c. plum preserves
1/4 c. onion, finely chopped
1/4 c. apricot preserves
2 Tbsp. brown sugar
2 Tbsp. apple cider or juice
2 Tbsp. soy sauce
2 Tbsp. ketchup
1 garlic clove, minced

Preparation:
1. In a small saucepan, combine all ingredients.
2. Cook over low heat, stirring occasionally, to allow flavors to blend.

5. Cooking Tips and Terms

Butter can be substituted with margarine.
Do not add salt when cooking mushrooms.

Beat: Rapid movement with a fork, spoon, wire whisk, or electric mixer to combine ingredients.
Blend: To combine ingredients until just mixed.
Boil: To heat liquids until bubbles form that cannot be stirred out.
Dash: A small amount of seasoning, less than 1/8 teaspoon.
Dredge: To coat food with flour or other ingredients.
Fold: To incorporate several ingredients by careful and gentle turning with a spatula, spoon, or whisk.
Mince: To cut into very fine pieces. A technique most often used for garlic or fresh herbs.
Puree: To process food to a smooth mixture. This can be done in an electric blender, food processor, or food mill or by pressing food through a sieve.
Sauté: To fry quickly in a small amount of fat, stirring almost constantly. A technique most often used to cook onions, mushrooms, and other chopped vegetables.